A Trip Through Time

by Cynthia Mercati

Cover Illustration: Clint Hansen
Inside Illustration: Dan Hatala

PB ISBN-10: 0-7891-5190-1 ISBN-13: 978-0-7891-5190-2
RLB ISBN-10: 0-7807-9510-5 ISBN-13: 978-0-7807-9510-5
Printed in the U.S.A.

6 7 8 9 10 11 PP 13 12 11 10 09 08

Contents

1

The Door to the Past

I was so bored I could have screamed!

No, it was worse than that. I was so bored I'd have cleaned the kitchen without being asked. Scrubbed the bathroom. Read a math book. I was so bored I could've played with my sister's Barbie dolls!

"Max!" My grandmother nudged me with her elbow. "Max, your grandfather asked you a question."

I blinked at my grandmother. I felt as if I were coming back from a trip to some far-off planet.

"Huh?" I said. I knew I sounded as clueless as I felt. But Grandpa just gave me a wink.

"It's okay, Max," he said. "A 12-year-old boy can get pretty antsy being cooped up with no one to talk to but his little sister and two adults."

How right that was!

My sister and I were spending a few weeks of summer vacation at my grandparents' house. For a while it had been great. I'd hung around with Grandpa in his toolshed, gone fishing, and built a fort in the backyard. And I'd stuffed myself with all the good food Grandma made.

But now I was starting to miss my pals back home. Sitting at the kitchen table with my grandparents just wasn't the same.

"I was just asking what you'll be studying in school next year," Grandpa said. His voice still carried more than a hint of a Norwegian accent.

"Oh . . . things," I said. I was still trying to come back to Earth from that bored-out-of-my-gourd planet I'd been on.

"Things," Grandpa echoed. And then he laughed. He had a great laugh—loud and deep. It seemed to start somewhere down in his belly and then just kind of bubble up to the surface. When I was a little kid, I used to think that was how Santa Claus must sound!

"I remember studying 'things' too," Grandpa said finally, when his laughter eased up. "Way back when!"

"I bet you didn't study them on a computer," I said and grinned. I speared another chunk of chocolate cake.

"You're right," Grandpa said. "I don't so much know of computers."

Sometimes my grandparents still got their English mixed-up or backward. And it always made me smile. Sometimes Grandma even called Grandpa "Big Kris." That had been his nickname back in Norway. He'd been taller than everybody else and really strong. And he was still that way.

"Are you studying anything of history then, Max?" Grandma asked as she wiped up the cake crumbs I'd spread all over the table.

I groaned inside. So loudly, in fact, I was sure the sound would come bursting right out of my ears. Or maybe explode right out of the top of my head! I was sure everyone had heard it. Including Grandma's fat gray cat that was sleeping on top of the refrigerator. And my mom and dad back in Des Moines!

Please don't ask me about history, I thought. No, no, NO! Because no matter how I answered, Grandma would say the same thing. "Your grandfather has some interesting history of his own to tell! Tell Max some of your stories, Kris!"

And then Grandpa would be off. Traveling back through time to before VCRs and video games. To back even before TV! He'd start telling me all about Norway and World War II. And how he'd spent his boyhood fighting the Nazis.

It didn't have to be a question about history that set Grandpa off, though. It could be a word. A thought. A movie. Anything that reminded him of the old days. And there was so much that reminded him!

The first time I heard Grandpa's stories, I thought they were really exciting. And even kind of scary. But back then I thought the Wicked Witch of the West in *The Wizard of Oz* was scary too. And the stepmother in *Cinderella*.

But I was a seventh grader now. And Grandpa's stories were . . . well—they were boring! World War II was so long ago not even my parents could remember it. And they're as old as dirt! They're so old, they were hippies in the '60s. With love beads and bell-bottoms! (I've seen the pictures!)

But Grandpa was already settling back in his chair. His snapping blue eyes were getting that faraway look. When he folded his arms over his stomach, I knew he was ready to begin. And I knew just how he'd start too. *"I was only a boy when the Nazis took over Norway. But my friends and I did all we could to stop Hitler!"*

What a snooze! I knew that when he was talking, I

couldn't just get up and leave. I'd tried that once. But Mom had pulled me back into the room. Later, she'd given me the lecture of my life about how rude I'd been.

But I just couldn't sit there and listen. Not one more time! If I did, I'd fall asleep right at the table. My head would clunk right down in the middle of the cake. I had to find a way out!

My sister was sound alseep in the bedroom. Taking her afternoon nap, the lucky duck. Little kids got all the breaks. I would've taken a nap too, if I'd known Grandpa was going to start in on his stories.

Maybe I could run an errand or wash the car. Or walk the dog. (My grandparents didn't have a dog. But maybe I could run out and buy one and then walk it.) Where was an escape pod when you needed one? I thought. Or an escape hatch, or an escape ship or—

"Max," Grandma said, "would you run up to the attic and—"

Would I?! I jumped up and was out of the kitchen in a flash. As I started up the stairs, my grandma's voice floated up after me.

"Bring down the scrapbook. It's very big and has a green cover. There are some pictures in there of Norway and Grandpa's old friends."

I took the stairs two at a time. Then I stopped at the attic door to catch my breath.

Wow! That had been close! One more minute and I would've been a goner. Grandpa's story would've started, and there would have been no turning back.

I pushed open the door. And I was immediately plunged into gloom. I searched around with one hand for the string that was hanging down from the ceiling. When I finally found it, I pulled on it. A single lightbulb blinked on. I could see swirling flecks of dust that tickled my nose.

My nose wrinkled too, at the smell that surrounded me. The smell of things that nobody had used for a long time. The smell of the past.

My mom's old bicycle leaned against one wall. And her old high chair stood next to it. It was so weird to think of my mom as a baby!

There was a big trunk too. It was filled with the old clothes and hats my sister used for her dress-up games. (I have to admit, I played with the same stuff when I was a little kid!)

There was a chair with a missing leg that Grandpa had been meaning to fix for years. A beat-up old table sat along one wall. And in one corner was an old mattress.

I wandered over to the mattress and felt it. It was a little lumpy. But not too bad. Maybe I should just lie down and take a little snooze. By the time I woke up, Grandpa might have forgotten about telling his stories.

Of course, the sight of the scrapbook would probably just start him off again.

I gave another groan—this time an out loud one! But still, I had to at least try to find the scrapbook.

I walked to the bookcase. That would be the logical place to look for it. There was a big cobweb hanging over one end. I swatted it away. Then I started looking over the books.

They were all old—of course!—and really dusty. I saw a couple of my mom's old storybooks and a couple of books that were written in Norwegian. But no scrapbook.

Oh, well, I thought. The longer it took me to find it, the longer I had an excuse for staying up here. The only trouble was, I really wanted out of this attic.

Maybe all the cake I'd eaten was fogging up my head with sugar. But I was starting to feel weird. Not sleepy—just kind of fuzzy. Like my brain was spinning backward.

But what else could I expect? Coming into this attic was like stepping into a time machine set on the past!

I suddenly saw a door way off in the back corner. It looked like it led to a closet. Funny, in all the times I'd been in this attic, I'd never noticed that door before. But then, it was kind of shadowy up here.

I walked to the door. As I did, a strange tingle ran up and down my backbone. I shivered.

Must be all the dust, I thought. Man, I'd be glad to get out of this place and into the sunlight again. This attic was really creeping me out!

I put a hand on the knob and turned. But the door wouldn't open. I shoved as hard as I could, but the door wouldn't budge. Probably the wood had warped from time and the weather. And now it was permanently stuck.

Well, if the scrapbook was in there, I wasn't going to find it. And that was okay with me. More than okay—it was great! Without the old pictures to remind him of his past, maybe Grandpa would give up on the stories and just take me fishing.

Just then the door flew open. It happened so suddenly and with so much force, it was as if the wind had done it.

But there was only one window in the attic. And it was tightly shut.

So then how—

Forget it, Max, I told myself sternly. It doesn't matter how the door came unstuck. The important thing is, it did! Just get in there, look for the scrapbook, and get out.

I reached into the closet and searched for a light switch or a string. But I couldn't find either one.

I stepped inside. Using both hands, I searched around the closet. But it was empty. No shelves, no hangers, no clothes or furniture. Only black nothingness.

I took another step, still searching. Then another . . .

Suddenly a blast of fresh air hit my face, and a breeze ruffled my hair. I was outside! I looked up, and a full moon met my eyes. It moved in and out from behind ragged clouds.

How had I gotten here? I hadn't come down any steps. And how come it was night? It had been afternoon when I left the kitchen. And if it was night, how come the streetlights weren't on?

I whipped my head around. The streetlights weren't on because they weren't there! And neither were the streets. Or the neighbors' houses—or my grandparents' house. I was surrounded by pine trees!

"I have a feeling we're not in Kansas anymore, Toto," I muttered out loud.

Then a new thought hit me. A dream! That's what this was! I'd lain down on the cot and fallen asleep. With such a full stomach, I was in one whopper of a dream.

I let out a sigh of relief. I made a fist and thumped myself on either side of my face. "Come on, Max, old man," I commanded myself. "Wake up!"

But I didn't. I lifted one foot and then set it down again. The earth definitely felt solid. I looked up. The moon, the clouds, the sky—they all looked very real. Too real to be a dream.

What was going on?! Had I wandered into a parallel universe? Or maybe I'd stepped over into another dimension. Yeah, that must be it! I was in another dimension. Things like that were always happening to the folks on *Star Trek*.

How could I get back? I thought. I hadn't moved an inch. Maybe I could just step backward into the closet again.

But when I tried, it was still night. And I was still outside.

I turned around and started feeling the air with both hands, palms up. I must look like one of those mimes trying to get out of the box, I thought. I started punching and poking at the empty air. I had to find that closet!

"Come on, come on," I muttered. "You've got to be there. There was a way into this place—there's got to be a way out!"

But there wasn't.

2

The Raid

"We're over here!"

The hoarsely whispered words had come from behind a huge pine tree. Its dead brown needles looked sharply different from the dark green trees around it.

Who was *we?* And why were they calling to me? I wondered.

A tall boy moved out from behind the tree and started toward me. Two other boys were behind him. They were all dressed alike—black pants, black sweaters, and black fisherman-type stocking caps. Their faces were blackened with what looked like burnt cork. All of them appeared to be about my age.

"You're right on time," the tall boy said.

Whoever I was, at least I was punctual!

"You were waiting for me?" I asked. Maybe if I played detective and asked some questions, I could find out a few things.

"Of course we were," the boy answered. "We got the word yesterday that someone from your Resistance unit would be joining our group in time for the raid tonight."

Resistance unit? Raid? Wherever I was, it sounded like something right out of *Star Wars!* The next thing I knew, the boys would be telling me about the Death Star and Darth Vader!

The tall boy stuck out his hand. "I'm Anders, the leader of this unit." He pointed in turn to the two other boys. "This is Ivor and Olav."

I shook Anders' hand. "I'm Max," I managed to say.

"This dead tree is a landmark around here," Anders said. "That's why we had you meet us here. If anyone ever gets separated while we're on a mission, this is the place to come and wait."

Olav's round face split into a wide grin. "We're really going to cause some trouble tonight! We'll make the Nazis sorry they ever invaded our country!"

Nazis?! Invasion?! It wasn't another dimension I'd landed in, it was another time—World War II!

But it wasn't World War II America. That I knew. The Nazis had never invaded our country. So which country was I in? And why hadn't the boys noticed how differently I was dressed?

Quickly, I looked down. And I discovered I was no longer wearing a T-shirt and baggy shorts. Instead, I wore the same clothes as the three boys. I touched my head. Yup, I had on a stocking cap too. I touched my face and wasn't surprised when black cork came off in my hands.

I figured we must be dressed like this for the raid they'd talked about. So we'd blend into the shadows. Either that or we were cat burglars!

Anders lifted one hand, as if giving a command. "We'd better get going. The truck will be waiting!"

With that, Anders started running. He had a loose, long-limbed stride that would have been the envy of our school's track team. The other two fell in behind him.

I started running too. What else could I do? I couldn't just stand there until I started growing roots.

The path we followed led through a thick forest. And it seemed to be all uphill!

Now let's get this straight—I am one tough dude. Well, one semi-tough dude. I don't mean I can pound in nails with my forehead or bend steel or anything. But I'm no wimp. I do play baseball and lift weights. (Well, once in a while I lift weights.) But these three guys set a pace that had me huffing and puffing. They could have run in the Boston Marathon!

I did my darndest to keep up with the other three. But it wasn't easy. As I ran, I took in lungfuls of clean air. Full of the scent of pine trees.

There was another scent in the air too. It wasn't one that we had in Iowa. But I had smelled it the summer our family had gone to Cape Cod on the Atlantic Ocean. I was almost sure it was the crisp, salty smell of the open sea!

Okay, Sherlock, I told myself, start putting the pieces of this puzzle together. The place where you are is close to the ocean, has been invaded by the Nazis, and has lots of pine trees and not a lot of people.

We came to a halt right about then. Thank goodness! My legs felt like rubber, and sweat was pouring off me. But the other guys were barely breathing hard. Maybe they were androids!

"Are you okay, Max?" Underneath all the burnt cork darkening his face, I could see Anders' concern. "They told us you went through the same kind of commando training we did. So I didn't think the run would bother you."

I managed to gasp out a few words about feeling just fine. Then I mentally kicked myself for taking it easy in gym class. If I was going to make it in this world—wherever it was—I was going to have to get physically fit in a hurry!

A kind of rumbling cut through the silence. A pickup truck came out of the darkness. I'd never seen a truck that old before, except in parades and movies. Why, I wondered, didn't the truck have its lights on?

Then I realized that it was trying to fade into the night. Just like we were.

Without a word, the three boys scrambled into the back. Gratefully, I followed them. At that moment I didn't much care where we were headed. As long as I didn't have to run!

The moon was still racing in and out of the clouds. But every once in a while, it threw off enough light so I could study the three boys.

Anders was thin, with a strong chin that gave him a proud, determined look. Olav, the short, round one, had a smile that didn't quit. And a lock of red hair kept falling out from under his stocking cap. When Ivor took his cap off to scratch his head, I saw he had brownish hair. He had brownish eyes too and a medium build. Just your ordinary, average-looking kid—like me!

But wasn't that what Grandpa had said about the Resistance fighters? That they were just average people? Both young and old, men and women?

I lay back in the truck bed and tried to remember what else Grandpa had told me. He'd said Resistance groups had been formed in every country the Nazis had conquered. France, Holland, Norway, Sweden, Denmark, and a few others I couldn't remember.

The Resistance did everything they could think of to give the Nazis trouble. Some groups, Grandpa had told me, had done big, dangerous things. Like blowing up railroad lines and stealing guns. Other groups had tried smaller things. Like switching street signs to confuse the Nazis.

I wondered what we were going to do that night. Maybe it would be something small. But maybe not.

My stomach started to feel a little jumpy. The way it did after I'd been on a roller coaster. These other guys had trained for whatever it was we were up to. But I hadn't!

Steve was my best friend back home. When we were just little squirts, we'd sometimes pretended we were big, bad soldiers off on a dangerous mission. It had all been fun and games back then. But this was the real thing!

If I ever saw Steve again, I knew what I was going to tell him. Stick to the make-believe. It's a lot easier on the stomach.

"There it is," Anders said suddenly. He pointed to a large building that looked like some kind of factory.

"That's where the Nazis make parts for their V-2 bombs."

There were no lights on or around the building. Probably to try to hide it from bombing raids by the English and Americans, I thought. I remembered from history class that our country and England had joined together to fight Adolf Hitler and Germany.

"Tonight we'll show the Germans just what we Norwegians are made of!" Ivor said proudly.

"We've been showing them," Olav added. "They'll never be able to make Norway knuckle under!"

Norway! That's where I was! Norway! Boy, that closet or time machine or whatever the heck it was sure had a sense of humor! I thought I'd escaped from Grandpa's stories. But instead, I was set down smack-dab in the middle of one!

Somehow I'd shown up at the right place and the right time to meet up with a Resistance unit. I was even wearing the right clothes! And since the boys could understand me and I could understand them, I must even be speaking Norwegian! It was all very weird. It was almost as if I'd been put here for a reason. . . .

The truck rumbled to a stop in front of the factory. The four of us jumped out. Two men walked toward us. They were dressed as we were. No one wasted time on introductions. I got the feeling that everything on this night had been timed down to the last second.

One of the men kept a watchful eye on the building. And the other man spoke to us.

"We tied up the guards," he said. "We took them far enough from the factory so they'll be out of danger when the explosives go off."

He handed Anders and Ivor each a can with a long spout on it. He gave a flashlight to Olav and me. "Work in pairs," the man said. "One of you hold the flashlight while the other one pours out the kerosene. Make straight lines from the door to the center beams. That's where we put the explosives. Who's going to light the fuse?"

"I am," Anders said. His voice was casual, as if he were volunteering to go out for pizza.

The man nodded. "You're really going to have to run to make it out in time. That goes for all of you. That stuff goes up fast."

"Don't worry," Olav said. "We've been through this before!"

Not all of us, I thought grimly. But I kept my lip firmly zipped. There just wasn't any explanation that wouldn't sound like I was one taco short of a combo platter.

No, I just couldn't picture myself saying, "See, guys, I was wandering around my grandparents' attic. And I got zapped back through time! I'm not a Resistance fighter. I'm just a seventh-grade schmo from Roosevelt Middle School!"

"Remember," the man warned, "it only takes one time to slip up."

The man's deadly serious words made me gulp. The sick feeling was back in full force. It felt like giant butterflies were zooming around in my stomach, head butting one another!

"We'll keep a lookout," the man said. He looked down at his watch. I noticed that the dial lit up so he could read it in the dark. "We've got just 15 minutes before the next shift of guards comes on duty. You'd better get to work." He gave us a salute. "Good luck!"

I was glad I was holding the flashlight. That was obviously the easiest job. As I held the light, Anders poured straight lines of kerosene. He went across the factory toward the center beam. Just as we'd been told.

Once we were done, Ivor, Olav, and I raced out of the building like someone was chasing us. We jumped into the truck. It seemed like forever, waiting for Anders. But I think it was probably only about a minute.

As soon as Anders was safely in the truck, the two men jumped in too. The driver had kept the engine running. And he took off like a drag racer.

We had only gone what would have been about two blocks back home. And suddenly an explosion shook the ground. The force of it almost threw us out of the truck.

The two men raised their fists. Olav and Ivor

shouted in triumph. Anders looked at me and flashed a quick smile.

"That was for Norway," he said. Then I heard him whisper to himself, "And for my father."

One of the men reached down under some canvas. He pulled out a handful of mean-looking nails. He threw them out of the truck. "That should slow down any Nazi car or motorcycle that tries to follow us!"

For a minute I glowed with pride. Then those head-butting butterflies in my stomach really went into action. I'd just had the adventure of my life! But I had the feeling there was a lot more to come. Would I be up to it?

3

For Freedom!

The truck reached the big pine tree with the brown needles. And the four of us jumped out. We walked a while through the trees. Then Olav and Ivor turned off the path to head for their homes. Both of them called out the same thing in farewell. "See you at the meeting tomorrow!"

"Your unit leader told you that you'd be staying with me, didn't he?" Anders asked. I nodded, and Anders went on. "We can go to the big meeting together."

I wondered what this big meeting was about. I wondered too, what else I was supposed to know that I didn't!

Anders' house was made of wood. It looked more like a cabin to me. It was small but comfortable.

His mother had the same kind of determined face that Anders did. She didn't say much. But she gave us both a big plate of food. Like the house, our meal was plain but good! I was sure the fish must have been caught that day. And the bread was homemade.

Anders introduced me as a friend in the Resistance. And his mother didn't ask any questions. After Anders and I ate our fill—and then some!—we climbed a ladder to the loft where he slept.

"You can take the bed," he said. "I'll be okay on the floor."

There was a jug and basin on a little table. I watched as Anders poured water from the jug into the basin and used it to wash up. After he finished, I did the same. Then he said he was going outside for a minute. It suddenly dawned on me that this house didn't have indoor plumbing!

When Anders came back, I made my trip through the dark to the outhouse. It was dark inside. And outside the door, I could hear animals scratching and stirring. (Small animals, I hoped!) All in all, though, it wasn't too bad. But it wasn't too good either.

Luckily, this was summer. I didn't even want to think what a trip to the outhouse would be like in the middle of a wild Norwegian winter. Snow beating down on my head and the wind whipping around my ankles. But if I didn't find a way out of the past, I wouldn't just be thinking about it—I'd be doing it!

On my way back to the house, I decided I had to get more information about this world I'd tumbled into. I climbed into bed. I plumped up the feather pillow and smoothed out the feather comforter. Then I called down to Anders.

"If you're not asleep yet, Anders, I'd like to ask you a few things. About how the Resistance is set up—" I stopped suddenly. I was glad it was dark so Anders couldn't see me pound myself on the head with the pillow!

You're supposed to know this stuff already, I scolded myself. Now think, man, think. Come up with a better way to put it.

Quickly, I went on. "What I mean is, they explained it all to me back home, of course. But I—uh—I wasn't listening too well. I kind of forgot."

"The Resistance divided Norway into eight districts," Anders answered. "Each one has its own chief. Under each chief are the individual groups—or units—of about four or five. The leaders of those groups report to the chief of their district. And he reports to the head man of all the districts, Captain John Rognes."

"Right, right," I mumbled. I was trying to sound like I'd heard all this before. "Now I remember."

"My father joined the Resistance right away," Anders went on. "He was so angry when the Nazis invaded Norway! His unit did everything they could to drive the Nazis crazy. They punctured the tires on their motorcycles and sank their ships. They even stole their guns! Every morning the Nazis play a record of the German national anthem in our village hall. Well, one day my father and his men stole their record. And they replaced it with a record of the Norwegian national anthem!"

I could hear the pride in Anders' voice. And something else too—a steely stubbornness.

"My father had a motto," Anders said. " 'Nothing is too little to do to the Nazis, and nothing is too great to try!' I've made that my motto too. I'm the leader of our little unit of three. Our district chief thought we needed another member. So that's why you were sent here."

He looked up and gave me a quick, approving nod. "You didn't ask any questions tonight. You just did your job and got out of there. You kept a good head on your shoulders."

What looked like *calm*, I knew was *fear.* But I

decided to let Anders think I was a cool dude, instead of a scared one!

For a moment Anders was quiet. When he spoke again, his voice was low. "About two months ago the Nazis ambushed my father's unit. The other men told me what happened. My father instructed them to run while he kept the Nazis busy. The others got away. They're hiding out up in the north now—in the mountains.

"But the Nazis caught my father," Anders continued. "They marched him into the square and stood him up against the village hall. Then they made everyone in town come out and watch. The Nazi commandant asked my father if it was true that he had been working with the Resistance."

Anders drew a deep breath. With one hand, he pushed a lock of black hair from his face. Then he went on. "My father said, 'Yes, it's true! And if I had to do it all over again, I'd do the same thing! Even knowing it would end this way. This is our country, and you have no right to it!' My father looked right at me then, and at my sister and mother. 'Fight on!' That's what he called out to us. 'Don't give up until Norway is free again!' The Nazis shot him before he even finished his last word . . . ."

Anders' voice caught and broke. And I heard him sniffle. I knew he was trying hard not to cry.

"I'm sorry, Anders," I said. My words sounded

hollow. And I felt silly even saying them. They weren't big or grand enough for this moment. But they were all I could think of.

"The very day the Nazis killed my father," Anders said, "I joined the Resistance. If anything happens to me, my sister will join up. We've made a promise to each other to honor Father's words. To fight on until Norway is free again!"

Anders lay back down then. The red curtained window was open to catch a cool night breeze. There was no noise except the occasional cry of a bird and the wind in the trees.

It was pretty quiet in my grandparents' small town too. But at least you could hear the cars going up and down the road. And maybe a radio or TV blaring away.

It was so quiet here I couldn't sleep! I just lay there and thought about the family living in this tiny house in this small village. And how brave they were. I thought about Olav and Ivor too. And the men who'd helped us carry out the raid. They were plenty brave too! It wasn't the make-believe bravery you saw in the movies. This was the true bravery of real people.

Anders, Ivor, Olav . . . they were my age. The same age as my friends back home. What would my friends and I do if an enemy army—as evil as the Nazis had been—invaded our country? How would we feel if those invaders marched into our town? Down our streets? How would we feel if we had to sing their anthem, salute their flag, and follow their rules? How would it feel to be puppets on a string, jerked this way and that by the Nazis?

If that ever did happen in the United States, I'd like to think that my friends and I would form ourselves into a Resistance unit. I'd like to think that we'd fight for freedom too!

Freedom . . . always before it had just been a word. But now I was starting to understand what it meant.

Thinking about my friends made me homesick. All at once I was really lonely for my own house. The kids at school. My mom and dad. My hamster. Even my sister!

In a minute I was going to start sniffling too. Quickly, I clamped my mouth shut, closed my eyes, and held my breath. That's what I'd done when I was a little kid and didn't want to cry. I hoped it would work now.

4

Code Name *Fridtjof*

Fridtjof—that's what the big meeting was about the next day. But it wasn't a *what*. It was a *who*. And it wasn't exactly about him. It was about a special mission he was in charge of.

"Fridtjof is his code name," Anders explained as we walked through the thick woods on the way to the meeting. "His real name is Captain Johan Olsen. He's the bravest and the greatest of all the Norwegian Resistance fighters!"

Anders peered at me then, puzzled. "How come you've never heard of him?" he asked.

"Uh—well—my village is pretty far away from things," I stuttered. "We don't get much news up there."

A few minutes later we were joined by Olav and Ivor. Soon all three boys were telling me stories about Fridtjof.

Olav told about how once a Nazi commandant had been awaiting an important shipment of weapons and ammunition. But Fridtjof and his men had hijacked the train. They replaced the ammunition with fruit. And then they sent *that* on its way to the commandant.

Ivor told me about how Fridtjof and his men had stolen Norway's entire supply of gold. They had taken 80 tons of gold bullion right from under the noses of the Nazi guards! Then they'd smuggled it across Norway and out of the country. And they'd given it to the English so Hitler couldn't get his hands on it!

Anders told me that Fridtjof and his men had helped keep up Norway's fighting spirit. "Everyone," he said, "takes courage from their courage!" Anders also told me that wherever and whenever Fridtjof and his men struck, they wrote the code name of their leader in big, bold letters. *FRIDTJOF!!*

"It gives the Nazis fits," Olav said. Then he flashed that megawatt grin.

"The Nazis want to capture Fridtjof more than anyone else in Norway," Ivor added. "He's taking a big risk by coming here to tell us about his next mission. It must be an important one."

From the way my three new friends talked about this Fridtjof, I was expecting a combination of Hulk Hogan and Zorro!

The four of us joined about 20 other people in a small shack deep in the forest. I wondered how they all had managed to find their way to such a well-hidden place. I wondered even more how we'd ever find our way out!

Men and women were there. Also a few kids that looked even younger than the four of us. We were all gathered together. All of us waiting for Fridtjof. Lookouts were posted at the one window and at the door. I was sure there would be guards outside too, keeping a silent watch.

I kept my own eyes on the door. Any minute, I thought, a man about seven feet tall with bulging muscles would come charging in! Maybe he'd even carry a sword and carve out his name on the wall!

But when he finally arrived, I saw that Fridtjof looked pretty much like all the other guys in the room. In fact, he looked like a guy you might see walking down any street in Des Moines! The mighty Fridtjof could have walked right past me at Wal-Mart, and I wouldn't have given him a second glance!

Anders, Olav, Ivor, and now Fridtjof . . . I was beginning to realize that the Resistance was made up of ordinary people who did extraordinary things!

I thought about the pictures I'd seen, in magazines and books, of the American soldiers who fought in World War II. They looked like pretty average guys too. But they'd done some very "un-average" things. All to save our country and the world from a bully named Hitler.

Fridtjof stepped to the center of the room. He was silent a moment, as if gathering his thoughts. When he started talking, everyone leaned forward eagerly.

"The first thing I want to say to everyone is thank you," he began. "Your country is grateful for all of your bravery and hard work. The Nazis invaded Norway and thought we'd just roll over and play dead. Well, we've certainly shown them they were wrong about that!"

A cheer went up from the whole room. Smiling, Fridtjof held up a hand for silence. "I know too," Fridtjof continued, "that many of you have lost friends and family to our cause, as I have. My sorrow is yours. But always remember, they would want us to fight on. And that's just what we're going to do! Remember, too, that no matter how long and hard the road to victory seems, right is on our side. We will win!"

At this, there were smiles of agreement. And nods. Everyone here knows how difficult it will be to whip the Nazis, I thought. But no one is giving up!

"We tie up Nazi soldiers trying to stop our Resistance," Fridtjof said. "And the more, the better. Because that means they will have fewer troops to fight against England and the United States. By keeping the Nazis busy here, we're not just fighting for Norway's freedom. We're fighting for the freedom of the whole world!"

I felt a glow of pride at Fridtjof's words. The night before I'd been one of those people helping Norway and the world! What I'd done had been very little. But it had been something.

Fridtjof began speaking again. Now I leaned forward too, taking in his every word.

"You all know that the city of Trondheim is not very far from here. In Trondheim, the *Gestapo* has taken over a building. In that building, they're working nonstop to try to break the Resistance. They have men trying to break our code for sending messages. Other people are trying to discover our radio signals.

"In the basement," he continued, "they torture the captured Resistance fighters. They keep torturing them until they either break down and give the Nazis information or die. In the attic is where the Nazis keep their prisoners."

Fridtjof paused. His face got very serious. His dark

brows drew together. When he went on, his voice had taken on real force. "That's why I've come here today. To get volunteers to help my unit rescue those prisoners!"

Gestapo—I remembered that word from history class. We had watched a movie about World War II that was actually pretty cool. And it showed some of the Nazi secret police. Our teacher had told us they were called the "Gestapo," and the word stuck in my head.

Wow, I thought, that was going to be some heavy-duty mission. Breaking prisoners out of a Gestapo stronghold! I wondered what the plan was. But in his next breath, Fridtjof told me.

"The British Air Force—the R.A.F.—will fly a bombing raid. This will, of course, distract the guards. It will also give us ten minutes to get inside, get up to the attic, free the prisoners, and get them outside. Then the R.A.F. will fly over again to give us enough cover to get the prisoners to safety."

There was a minute of silence. I could tell that Fridtjof's words were just sinking in. Even to my untrained ears, it sounded like a real gamble!

"It sounds pretty impossible!" Olav shouted out.

"It *is* almost impossible," Fridtjof said. And then he smiled. His grin was as big as Olav's. "But not completely impossible!" he continued.

Fridtjof then went on to explain how he'd smuggled out photographs of the Gestapo headquarters to Britain. He'd also smuggled out maps that showed the exact location of the Nazis' antiaircraft guns. The British had also been given a timetable of when the prisoners would be in their cells and not in the basement. Together, Fridtjof and the British Air Force had made their plan.

"It's a big risk," one of the women in the room said.

Fridtjof agreed. "It is that. But I think this is one risk we have to take! The men in that prison are our brothers in the Resistance. Wouldn't we want them to take the risk for us?"

"Of course we would!" someone shouted. Everyone else in the room nodded.

"This mission will be a dangerous one," Fridtjof said. "I can't promise that everyone who participates will come home safe. All I can tell you is how important it is."

His eyes roamed over the people who sat listening to him. "I need four volunteers. Is there anyone who will stand up—and help my unit free the prisoners?"

For a moment no one moved. Then suddenly, Anders leaped to his feet. Then Olav and Ivor stood up. And then I stood up. I was trying to look brave. But inside, all kinds of thoughts were running through my mind.

"Are you crazy?" one part of me was saying. "This isn't the movies. This is real life! Real Nazis will be coming after you!"

"Those three guys are your friends," the other part of me answered back. "Besides, weren't you wondering just last night what you'd do if the Nazis invaded your country? Well, now's your chance! You can prove to yourself that you're not just some junk food-munching, TV-watching wimp. But a guy who's willing to stand up for what he believes in!"

The other half of me still wasn't thrilled I was going on the mission. But at least it shut up long enough for me to get my instructions.

"Tomorrow you'll learn exactly what we'll be doing," Fridtjof said to the four of us. "The next day will be the mission. We have to move fast so word about what we're doing won't leak out."

He looked at each one of us. "All I can say is thank you for volunteering. Thank you from me—and Norway!"

Then Fridtjof started singing. Everyone else in the room stood up and joined in. I figured it must be the Norwegian national anthem. I didn't know the words, so I just kind of hummed along.

The sound got louder and louder. Everyone else singing and me humming away like some crazy canary! It got so loud, I was sure even old Hitler himself, sitting in Germany, could hear us!

5
The Mission

The day of our big mission dawned bright and clear. "A good morning for flying," Anders said happily as we started out of the house.

We hadn't told his mother where we were going. This was top secret. We couldn't breathe a word to anyone. But mothers, from Iowa to Norway, have some kind of super built-in radar. They always seem to know what their kids are up to.

Anders' mother said her good-byes and sent us off. But then she called her son back for a big hug. "Your father would be very proud of you," she whispered.

Then she stood framed in the doorway and watched us go.

"She knows, doesn't she?" I asked Anders in a low voice.

"She doesn't know exactly what we're doing," Anders answered. "But she knows it's for the Resistance."

"It must be hard for her," I said. I was thinking of my own mom. And how hard it would be for her.

"To have Norway free again is important to her too," Anders said. "Not just because of my father. But because she loves her country."

We met up with Olav and Ivor by the same big pine tree. In a few minutes a truck, driven by one of Fridtjof's men, picked us up. The four of us lay down flat in the truck bed. The driver covered us with a heavy canvas tarp. Then he piled on a bunch of crates and boxes. It had to look like the truck was carrying supplies and not people.

I was glad Trondheim wasn't very far away! The four of us had to stay perfectly still and make absolutely no sound. But the road was rough. As we bumped and thumped along, the rough edges of the crates and boxes dug into my back and pressed down on my legs.

I couldn't move so much as an inch to get more

comfortable. Just in case the Nazis should pick that moment to search the truck. No, all I could do was grit my teeth and try to get my mind on something else.

So as we bounced along, I went over everything that Fridtjof had told us the day before. I'd never paid such close attention to anything in my life!

I have to admit, I wasn't always the best student in class. In fact, most of the time I was a Class A1 goof-off! When the teacher was trying to explain something, I'd usually let my mind wander or stare out the window. Or whisper to the person next to me. One time I even drifted off to sleep. I snored so loud that the whole class—and the teacher—heard me!

If I blew a test, I'd just tell myself that it didn't matter. There would always be another one. If I got a bad grade on a report, I'd just think it was no big deal.

It wasn't that I didn't want to do well in school. It was just—well, that I was too lazy to try my hardest.

It seemed like every time I got a report card, the teacher wrote the same thing on it. "Max doesn't work up to his potential." Or, "Max would get better grades if he applied himself."

I knew it wasn't only my parents I'd let down. When I was assigned to a group project in school, I'd let everyone else do the work.

Even in Little League, I didn't do all that I could. Too often I'd let a ball go by in the field. One that I might have been able to catch if I'd just tried a little harder. Or when I ran the bases, I wouldn't always turn on the steam like I could have.

"Hustle, Max!" That's what my coach was always telling me. "Hustle!"

Well, today I knew I couldn't slack off or let someone else do the work. Maybe I'd been a careless student and a lazy baseball player. But I wasn't going to be a sloppy Resistance fighter! This time I wouldn't—couldn't—let anyone down.

This mission was a one-time thing. We'd only have one shot to rescue the prisoners. No one could afford to goof off for even an instant. This time Max Evans was going to hustle!

I could tell we were in Trondheim by the noise. I knew this city would be much smaller than the ones I was used to and have a lot less traffic. Still, I could hear the occasional rumble of a truck or car. I could hear the sounds of people too. It was weird hearing everything and not being able to see it.

At the sudden roar of a motorcycle, Anders nudged me. "Nazis," he mouthed.

The motorcycle sounded as if it were right next to us. Those head-butting butterflies in my stomach sprang into action again. I held my breath. I made myself not move a single muscle until the motorcycle moved off. Finally the truck came to a stop, and the tarp was pulled off.

According to plan, the truck was hidden in a clump

of bushes. The five of us jumped down. As quickly as we could, we hid in the bushes too.

Fridtjof and his men were already waiting. As the two groups blended together, Fridtjof pointed to a tall building striped in brown and green.

"That's it," he whispered. "Gestapo headquarters."

I stared at the building, as if trying to see through the brick and cement. It was U-shaped. Behind the building, hidden from the street, the two arms of the *U* encircled a courtyard. Inside the building, the Gestapo would be working to defeat the Resistance. Phones would be ringing. Typewriters would be clacking.

Down in the basement, the Gestapo would be trying to break the will and spirit of the Resistance fighters they'd captured. Fridtjof had told us that the Gestapo used machine gun straps to whip and slash the flesh of their prisoners. He'd told us too, that the victims' screams sometimes echoed out of the windows.

In front of the building, black-uniformed soldiers marched back and forth. They kicked their legs out high in front of them. And they held their backs straight. I could imagine their eyes staring out icily from underneath their helmets. And I could imagine their faces too. Hard and fearsome. Scaring off anyone who dared to pass by.

As I watched the soldiers moving like military robots, I swallowed a couple of times. I was trying to gulp down my nerves. How could our small band of volunteers stand up against such practiced soldiers? Would even Fridtjof's crack Resistance fighters be any match for them? Maybe we'd all end up prisoners in that dark building!

I bit my lips. I curled my hands into fists and then uncurled them again.

I felt a little bit like when I'd been in line to get on the Flying Dragon roller coaster at Adventureland— the biggest, scariest roller coaster ever invented! I'd wanted to go on it, and yet I hadn't. I'd wanted to prove I was brave enough to take a ride. And yet I was afraid that deep down, I really wasn't. And what I was about to do now would make the Flying Dragon look like the Duck Pond ride at Kiddieland!

Would I be able to measure up? Were Anders and Ivor and Olav—and Fridtjof—right to put their trust in someone like me, a seventh-grade klutz?!

"It's almost 11:00," Olav whispered. That was when the Germans made their daily test of the city's air raid sirens. The R.A.F. had chosen that time to make their first flyover. The sirens would block out the noise of the planes.

Eleven o'clock. That was when the mission would begin. Just a few more minutes. Could I do it? I started arguing with myself again.

"Of course you can do it, Max," one part of me was saying.

"Of course you can't," the other side was saying. "You were stupid to even try!"

"Give it a rest," I said to myself, shutting down both parts of me. "Now isn't the time for Monday morning quarterbacking. I don't have any choice. I *have* to do it!"

To get my mind off the time, I glanced at the men Fridtjof had brought with him. I was trying to see how they stacked up against those Gestapo guys.

And that was when I saw him.

He was half a head taller than anybody else. And poking out from underneath his black stocking cap were bright blond curls. He reminded me of someone, and in a big way. But I couldn't figure out who. I moved about half an inch and squinted my eyes, trying to get a better look.

The big guy looked to be about 14 or 15. And he had snapping blue eyes. Eyes like my grandfather!

My own eyes popped wide. It couldn't be! Or could it?! This guy looked about the age Grandpa would have been at this time. He was in the Resistance, just as my grandfather had been. He had the same blond hair I remembered seeing in pictures of my grandfather when he was young. He was as big as my grandpa too.

And then he laughed. A belly-shaking kind of laugh that no one but Santa Claus had. And my grandfather!

At a hissed whisper from Fridtjof, the big guy quickly clamped a hand over his mouth.

"Anders," I said quietly as I pointed to the boy. "Who is that? Do you know his name?"

"Sure," Anders whispered back. "That's Big Kris Nelsen. He's been with Fridtjof since the beginning."

Big Kris Nelsen. My jaw dropped open. I blinked. And then I blinked again. I shut my eyes and shook my head, trying to clear it. This couldn't be happening. It couldn't!

But when I opened my eyes, I was still looking at my own grandfather! How could I have been flung through the past and come out exactly at the same time and the same place as my own grandfather?! This was just too much of a coincidence!

But maybe it wasn't a coincidence at all. I'd wondered before if I'd been put here for a reason. Maybe I had! Maybe I hadn't just been flung through time like a Nerf ball! Maybe I'd been set down at this time and this place, with these people, for a specific purpose. And maybe that purpose had something to do with my grandfather.

At that moment the air raid siren went off. I couldn't spend any more time worrying or wondering why I was there. Now I had a job to do.

According to the plan, 18 British Mosquito bombers and 28 Mustangs, British fighter planes, should have been in the air for a while now. They'd be flying so low they'd be under the radar curtain and wouldn't be spotted.

Also according to plan, the Nazis would be done by now with their morning questioning of the prisoners. All 36 Resistance fighters would be back in their attic cells. The prisoners who could no longer walk, because of the torture, would be dragged up the stairs and flung facedown on the floor.

Through his network of spies, Fridtjof had discovered more about the prisoners. Those the Gestapo had been unable to get information from would be stood before a firing squad later that week. Which made it even more important that we get them out today. And get them out alive.

As the air raid sirens wailed away, the planes swept into view. The Mosquitos were formed into groups of six bombers each. The Mustangs guarded and guided each formation.

The planes were flying so low, it seemed like they were touching the roofs. The roar of their engines rattled windows and shook buildings on their foundations. They streaked across the sky so swiftly that their red, white, and blue R.A.F. markings were a blur. People in the streets stopped and stared. And then they ran for safety.

The leader of the first formation pointed the nose of his plane at the Gestapo headquarters. Close on his tail came the other five Mosquitos of the first wave. Then it was *bombs away!*

They were "skip bombing" the building, as they had told Fridtjof they would. Fridtjof had explained "skip bombing" to us. The bombardier would fire his missle at a set angle so that it would "skip" or skim like a flat stone on the surface of a lake.

The Mosquito bombardiers had calculated it all out. A 500-pound bomb dropped on the courtyard would skip through the first floor windows before exploding. The blast would crush the lower half of the building while sparing the top floor and the prisoners in their cells.

Nazi soldiers poured from the Gestapo building. They ran to man their antiaircraft guns. But the Mustang fighters darted here and there. They protected the Mosquitos with their machine gun fire. The Gestapo building rocked and swayed from the force of the explosions. Flames shot from the lower half.

The *rat-a-tat* of the guns, the blasts of the bombs, the fury of the fire—it was all crowding in on me. I couldn't think anymore. For a moment I forgot everything Fridtjof had told us. Everything I was supposed to do. I even forgot why I was there!

For that one moment I wanted to turn and run. Far away from the Gestapo building, my new friends, and my responsibilities.

Then I heard Fridtjof yelling. "We have ten minutes! Remember—only ten minutes to get the prisoners out!"

Anders jumped up from a half crouch and started running for the building. Ivor and Olav were on his heels. Of course, I wouldn't desert them now. Wouldn't and couldn't!

I stumbled to my feet and started running too. My legs were pumping. And my lungs were bursting from excitement and smoke.

The front door had exploded off its hinges. I followed the other Resistance fighters through the gaping hole. Those soldiers who weren't injured tried to stop us from entering. According to the plan, Fridtjof's men battled them back.

The four of us ran up the stairs and to the attic. Some of the cell doors had been blown open. Small groups of prisoners stood in the hallway. They were thin. And their clothes were ragged. Their faces and bodies bore the bruises of recent beatings. They stared at us as we burst up the stairs.

"We're with Fridtjof!" Anders yelled. "We're here to rescue you!"

Some of the prisoners cheered at that and grabbed our hands to shake them. But others were confused from the torture they'd been through and only looked blank.

Ivor ran up to those prisoners. He explained what was happening. Then he began leading them down the stairs.

At the far end of the hall, I saw a soldier who was

lying facedown. He must have been knocked unconscious by one of the explosions, I thought. Fastened to his belt was a huge ring of keys. I ran to him.

Without pausing to take a breath, I grabbed the key ring and ran to the closest cell. Fingers shaking, I tried key after key until I got to the one that unlocked the cell doors. I flung the first cell door wide open. Then I ran to the next one, and the next.

Olav and Anders followed me. They went into each cell and guided the prisoners out. Most of them were able to walk, although slowly and with effort. But a few couldn't even manage that. My friends helped those few out.

Two prisoners leaned heavily on Olav as he led them carefully down the stairs. The man who was leaning on Anders had bandages over his eyes.

I flung open the last cell. A man hobbled toward me. His face was screwed up in pain. It looked like it hurt him just to move. He had a big purple bruise on one temple. And one eye was almost swollen shut.

I ran to him and slid an arm under his shoulder. We stumbled toward the door and into the hall. The smoke was thicker now. Both the man and I were coughing. I wondered how much time was left before the second wave of Mosquitos would roar into Trondheim and finish off the Gestapo building.

But I couldn't wonder too much. All my effort had

to be used to get the prisoner down the stairs. We struggled forward.

"Come on," I encouraged him. "You can make it!"

"I don't think I can," the man gasped out. He was breathing heavily. His steps were slower and slower. "Go on," he said. He gave me a weak little shove. "Get out! Save yourself!"

I jutted out my chin. "We'll get out together!" I said firmly. But would we?

At the bottom of the stairs, my three friends were gesturing to me to hurry.

Anders started up the stairs. "I'll help you!" he yelled.

"No!" I waved Anders away. I waved them all away. "Get out!" I shouted. "Don't worry—we'll make it!"

My words sounded a lot more confident than I was. But I wouldn't leave the prisoner. And I couldn't let my friends risk their lives to help us.

The smoke was stinging my eyes. I swiped the back of one hand across my eyes to try to clear them. But all I did was leave a streak of soot on my face. I blinked a few times.

"Get going!" I shouted to the three boys below. But still they hesitated. I yelled again. "Get out—now! I'll meet you in the truck!"

Finally Olav gave me a grin and the thumbs-up signal. Ivor yelled, "We did it!" Then they ran outside.

I looked down at Anders. He was plainly undecided. "You have to make it out," I yelled at Anders. "You have to help the Resistance! Remember the promise you made your father! For a free Norway!"

Anders looked straight at me. He nodded. "For a free Norway!" he said. Then he disappeared through the hole that had been the doorway.

Slowly, slowly, the prisoner and I edged down the stairs. Time seemed to have stopped. It could have been ten minutes or twenty, one hour or two. Or a lifetime. I didn't know and didn't care. I concentrated all my energy on the prisoner.

Then suddenly, footsteps were pounding up the stairs. I looked up to see Big Kris Nelsen in front of me. "I'll take him," he said quickly.

Before I could protest, Big Kris bent over and flung the prisoner onto his back, fireman style. With his great height and strength, it didn't seem like an effort at all.

Kris, with the prisoner over his back, started down the stairs. I followed behind. I took a deep breath. I was going to make it out after all!

But at that moment a figure lying at the bottom of the stairs suddenly leaped up. He stood directly in front of us. It was a Gestapo man. His uniform was torn and burnt. And his eyes were hard in his soot-blackened face. He swung his rifle to his shoulder.

In a minute—no, less than a minute!—he would fire. I was the only one who could do something. But what?!

And then my eyes fell on the banister. Most of it had fallen away. But a few pieces of wood still stood up in jagged points.

I reached out and broke one of the biggest pieces off. I grasped the piece of wood with both hands. Putting my whole body into it, I flung the wood at the soldier. It hit him squarely on the head, knocking him down. He yelled in pain, dropping his gun. Thank goodness for Little League, I thought!

"Run!" I yelled to Big Kris. "Run! Before he gets up again!"

For someone so big—and someone weighed down with another person!—Kris was surprisingly quick. But just as he started outside, he turned back and flashed me a grin. "You saved our lives!" he shouted.

Wow, I thought, I just saved my own grandfather's life! But I still had to save my own.

I ran down the stairs. But the soldier I'd knocked down was getting to his feet again. Doing the best imitation of a kung fu fighter I could manage, I crashed both legs into him. Down he went. And out I went, into the fresh air!

I headed for the truck. Overhead, the second wave of Mosquitos and Mustangs was roaring toward the Gestapo building. I ran faster than I ever had in my life. I could hear the thunder of the planes and the crackle of the fire. I could hear the yells of my friends and the other Resistance fighters. Everyone was calling for me to hurry, hurry!

All the noises seemed to melt together. The red of the fire, the green of the grass, the blue of the sky all ran together too. The shapes, the sounds, the colors— everything mixed together. Whirling and swirling around and around in my brain.

And then I was whirling and turning. Spinning through darkness. I couldn't see anything. I couldn't hold onto anything. I felt like I was free-falling through the universe!

Suddenly, the spinning stopped. I was standing. I stuck my arms out, feeling my way through the blackness. I took one step and then another. And then I stepped out again into my grandparents' attic.

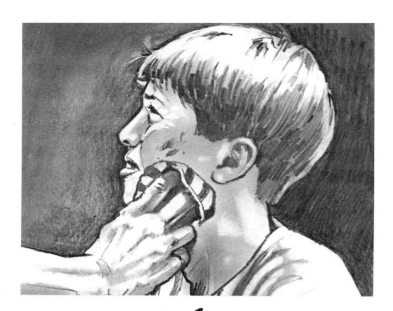

6

Back Home

I looked around. Yup, it was the same attic I'd been in before. I looked down. Yup, I was wearing the same old baggy shorts, T-shirt, and beat-up Nikes I'd had on before.

How had I gotten back here?

I quickly turned and looked for the door to the closet. It wasn't there. I started feeling along the wall with both hands. Maybe if I pushed hard enough, the wall would give way to reveal a secret door. And that door would lead to the closet.

But nothing happened. My time machine was gone. I fell back against the wall and pressed my hands to my head. Whirling, swirling thoughts were still charging around in my brain. But now they were memories of all the things I'd seen and done.

The sound of all the Resistance fighters singing the Norwegian national anthem. The quiet Norwegian night. Short, round Olav and his wide grin. Average-looking Ivor. Tall Anders with his determined face. Fridtjof! Talking with Anders in his little home. Bouncing along in the truck under that tarp. The raid on the factory. The raid on Gestapo headquarters!

My body was here in the present. But my brain was still out in the stratosphere somewhere! I couldn't quite make the leap back to my real life. Maybe if I would lie down for a minute . . .

I made a dive for the lumpy cot. I fell onto it with a *plop*. I lay back, hands folded behind my head. I shut my eyes.

"Come on, Max, old man," I said to myself, "get with it. Sure, you had a cool time fighting against the Nazis and being heroic and stuff. But you're back home now. You gotta snap out of this and pick up where you left off!"

But I didn't want to. I didn't want to go back to being the old Max, the lazy goof-off. I wanted to be the Max I'd been in Norway. The Max who'd done all he could for freedom. For his friends.

Sure, doing a group report or taking a test wasn't exactly like fighting the Nazis. But they were still duties. People were still depending on you to do all you could. And I was through being the guy you couldn't count on.

I decided that from now on, I wasn't going to let anyone down. Not my parents, not my friends. But most of all—not myself.

Oh, wow, I thought. I'd come up to this attic one person. But I'd go down the stairs another! And all because I'd stepped into a closet and taken a trip through time! It all seemed so crazy.

Except . . . the closet wasn't there anymore. Or maybe it had never been there. Maybe none of this had really happened at all. I was getting so confused.

I sat up slowly. Maybe I'd come into the attic, gone over to this cot, lain down . . . and everything from then on had been a dream.

Of *course* it had been a dream. What else could it have been! I must've just remembered one of Grandpa's stories and relived it in my dream. Even whacking myself on the face and telling myself to wake up had been part of the dream!

I groaned and fell back again. I was embarrassed that I was such a dope. How could I have thought I'd been whisked away in a time machine?

"Max," I whispered out loud, "you're an idiot. You just had a dream!"

"Max!" My grandmother's voice echoed up the

stairs. "What happened to you? You've been up there half an hour! Did you find the scrapbook? I think it's in the bookcase."

I scrambled to my feet. I'd only been sleeping half an hour?! Boy, I'd sure crammed a lot into a 30-minute dream!

I ran over to the bookcase for one more useless search. But wait a minute—wait a doggoned minute! There was the scrapbook on the bottom shelf. It was big and bulky with a green cover. Just like Grandma had described it. But I knew I'd looked down there before. Or had I?

Searching through the bookcase and even swatting away the big cobweb must have been part of the dream too!

I grabbed the scrapbook and stuck it under one arm. Without looking back, I ran out the door and down the stairs. As soon as I reached the kitchen, I looked out the window. Yup, it was still afternoon, and the sun was still shining brightly. Maybe the sunshine would clear out the crazy fog in my brain.

Grandpa was still seated at the table, drinking coffee. I looked at my grandfather in a way I never had before. Because now I realized he wasn't just a great guy with his booming laugh and those snapping blue eyes. He was a hero! A true hero, who'd risked his life not for glory or fame. But for his country.

I felt ashamed thinking about all the times I'd just

blown off his stories about the Resistance. Well, no more!

I sat down next to him. And the words tumbled out of me. "Grandpa, your stories—I mean your stories about Norway and the war and the Resistance—I want to hear them. All of them. Right from the beginning!"

Grandpa's forehead wrinkled. He looked like he was trying to figure out what I'd said. "I know you ran up to the attic so you wouldn't have to hear those old stories one more time, Max. And it's all right. An old man who just wants to talk about the past can be very boring."

How could I explain to Grandpa how I'd had a change of heart up in the attic? I couldn't. I'd just have to show him. And I'd have to start right now.

"Maybe I was kind of bored before," I began. "But now I'd really like to hear your stories. All of them! You know. About the raid on Gestapo headquarters in Trondheim with Fridtjof! And—"

I broke off. Grandpa was staring at me in a really strange way. His blue eyes were puzzled. "How did you know about that?" he asked. "I've never talked about that before."

"You must have," I answered. How else would I have known about it in my dream?

Grandpa shook his head. "No. It was so sad that I never wanted to talk about it," he said.

"It wasn't sad," Grandma said as she burst into the room. She didn't even look at us as she whirled through the kitchen, washing dishes and wiping up crumbs. "It was an amazing thing. The Resistance fighters rescued 36 prisoners. Thirty-six!"

"And Grandpa carried one of them down the stairs on his back," I broke in eagerly. I was anxious for him to continue the story I now remembered so well.

But Grandpa's frown only deepened. "How do you know these things, Max?" he asked.

"Oh, Kris," Grandma said with a sigh of impatience. I think she suspected Grandpa was getting a little senile! "He knows because you told him. How else would he know? You've just forgotten."

Grandpa opened the scrapbook. He turned the pages until he came to the one he wanted. He jabbed one finger at a small, faded black-and-white snapshot. "These are all the people who went on the Trondheim mission," he said.

I stared at the old picture. I pointed to each one in turn. "There's Anders and Olav and Ivor. And there's Fridtjof. And there's Grandpa—"

I sat back suddenly. I knew I had never seen this scrapbook before. So how did I know who was who? How did my dream know the faces for the names in Grandpa's stories?

Grandpa was wondering the same thing. He looked at me. He was blinking in bewilderment. "How do you know these people?" he asked me.

Grandma was still working away at the sink. She

called over her shoulder, "You're a better storyteller than you think, Kris. That's all! You must have told Max just exactly what everyone looked like."

I relaxed. Of course, that was it!

"There's just one person missing," Grandpa said. And there was a faraway sound in his voice. He was dipping back into the past again. "There was another volunteer, a friend to the other three boys you just mentioned. He saved my life. And the life of the prisoner I was carrying."

Grandpa paused. "He was killed. The only one we lost on the raid. That's why it's so sad. That's why I don't like to tell about it."

A chill ran up my spine. Tears formed in my eyes. *Killed?!* But I thought he'd gotten out. . . .

Grandpa must have told me about the raid sometime. Or else how would I have known enough to dream about it?

And it had to be a dream, I thought again. People do not just stumble into closets, fall back through time, and meet up with their own grandfather! That only happens in books or movies. And this wasn't either one. This was just the ordinary, everyday life of Max Evans!

Unless . . . and as this thought struck me, a chill ran up my spine again. The head-butting butterflies started running around my stomach again.

Maybe I *had* been sent back to the past. And sent back for a special reason. Maybe not being able to find the scrapbook had all been part of it. So that I'd go looking around and stumble into the closet. And so I'd be whisked away back to World War II Norway. Just in the nick of time to save Kris Nelsen's life!

My head was starting to spin again. There's no way I could've been sent to the past. Grandma must be right, I assured myself. Grandpa must've told me the story and just forgotten. I must've forgotten too. Actually, I probably was just spacing out when he told me. And only my subconscious mind remembered.

I decided to forget about my weird ideas and focus on learning more about my heroic grandpa.

I started turning the pages of the scrapbook again. "Come on, Grandpa," I said. "Tell me all about these people. Were they all Resistance fighters too? And how did you feel when the Nazis marched into Norway? And were you ever scared? And—"

Grandpa held up one hand for silence. And he laughed that great rumbling laugh. "One question at a time, Max. And one story at a time, okay?"

I laughed too. "Okay," I agreed.

Grandpa settled back in his chair. He folded his hands over his stomach. Just like he had done many times before. But this time, instead of groaning inside, I settled in too. I couldn't wait to hear what he was going to tell me!

And I couldn't wait to get back home either. Everyone was going to be so surprised. No more lousy report cards. No more letting a ball get by me. No, this new-and-improved Max Evans was going to give it all he had. All the time. And all thanks to a dream.

Just then Grandma turned from the sink. She stared at me for a moment. Then she walked over to me and started wiping at my face with a wet dish towel.

"Hey, what are you doing?" I asked as I squirmed away from her. I had flashbacks of when I was little. She would scrub my face so hard I was afraid she'd rub it all off.

Grandma shook her head like she was confused. As she continued to wipe my face, she said, "You've got a big smudge of soot on your face. As if you've been in a fire! How ever did you get soot on your face up in the attic?"

I felt the blood rush from my face. I couldn't speak to answer her. And I didn't even know *how* to answer her anyway.

Of *course* it was a dream—wasn't it?